Debt and Self-sufficiency

ZEN

Roditch Roditch

Contents

Introduction

I have lived through the 1950s and 1960s and have had personal experience of living cheaply. It was not my intention back then to be debt-free and live a sustainable life; it just turned out that way. My personal experience back then and my present situation in life both harken to the artist's life: soul searching where money seldom goes.

The divide between the rich and poor is growing exponentially. It is the age of "prosperity consciousness," where everyone has the God-given right to be filthy rich. I have always believed that as the rich get richer, the poor get poorer, and so it is. Leaders of governments around the world lead to further themselves and keep their power. They strive to be rich while taxing the poor. They are often puppets of oligarchs, governing for the rich, not the people.

Equivalent wages are a quarter of what they were in 1972. If you don't have the cash to build a home or buy a car, then you have to borrow it. Banks make a lot of profit from you these days because it's impossible to save money. For the average person, life is only sustainable through debt, entertainment, distractions, alcohol, sex, and religion—all of which are available in spades on the internet.

There is another way, which I will explain the best I can in this book. Like Richard Overton, I don't have a credit card, and I keep all my things forever. I avoid debt and pay cash for everything because I don't want to pay interest or sales tax to anyone. Rich people usually avoid paying interest and tax, and poor people are drowning in it. You don't have to decide if you want to be rich or poor. There is another way: you can decide to live a sustainable life where you are debt-free, grow your own food, and make most things you need, even your own home. There is quite some pride to be gained from this approach as well.

There are many reasons why it's good to be more self-sufficient and reduce your consumerism. We don't know the future: war, financial collapse, meteorites hitting the earth, climate change, robots, 5G wireless, censorship, increasing health and pharmaceutical costs (related to an increase in cancer and other health issues), other natural disasters, reduced personal freedom by authoritarian governments, lazy and dependent offspring, and education.

Life seems tough these days: 90% of Americans have no savings and enormous debt. This must change. Everyone needs to wake up, stop and think about what they are doing, and quickly reduce the collateral damage to their wallets.

Seven Plums – Li Ziqi

and self-sufficiency

Li Ziqi was born in the 1990s. She's a woman who lives in the deep mountains of Sichuan (Szechwan), China. Unlike other online celebrities, although she's famous on the Internet nowadays and always appears in beautiful clothes, Li Ziqi wore a modified version of Hanfu (a kind of Han Chinese traditional clothing) back then. She uses the most traditional methods and the most traditional tools but has a unique perspective on how to present Chinese traditional dishes to the world. She is a "Wonder Woman" in the eyes of her fans, as she can achieve things that normal people cannot.

Chinese people's traditional concept of family: the Taoist thought of harmony between man and nature.

Li Ziqi's grandfather was a cook working in the countryside. When there was a ceremony going on, be it a wedding or a funeral, her grandfather would be in charge. In the videos, she shows how to cook various dishes, which she learned from her grandfather. Besides cooking, she also learned how to make bamboo baskets, go fishing, grow vegetables, and do carpentry work from her grandparents. When she was young, she left her home to work in a city, then a few years ago she came home to take care of her sick grandmother. She started work early in the morning and returned home late. Like other farmers who earned their living on the farm, she was living an ordinary life in the countryside.

Li Ziqi is usually dressed as an ordinary young person living in a rural area, sometimes even more casually. Li Ziqi grows a lot of crops at home, such as popcorn and peanuts; she also needs to feed the pigs and raise silkworms, which is the major source of income for her family.

She lives in Sichuan province, which is known as the "Land of Heaven" in China. The land is fertile, and it is rich in resources. It has beautiful scenery and is located in Mianyang, the northwestern part of the Sichuan Basin, with Gansu in the north and the Sichuan Basin in the south. It has four distinct seasons and a wide variety of plants.

Li Ziqi uses farming, cooking, and handicraft skills she learned from her grandfather. As a modern young woman, she expands on that knowledge through the internet and her creativity. On her YouTube channel, she creates a sustainable life in China that millions of people love. She does make money from her channel, but her "idea" of a beautiful rural life—taking all the time you need to make your own clothes using natural fibers and dyes—is what makes her so successful. To collect all the ingredients for dinner from the fields and nearby mountains and slowly craft traditional and timeless Chinese dishes. She also made her own mud oven to bake bread and other foods. Her videos show the possibility, the joy, and the wonder of having time to live a simple life and enjoy every moment—quite different from living in an apartment and shopping at supermarkets every day.

The time is coming soon when our time will be worthless. For every hour we work, there will be an hour of bills to pay. Bills, including taxes and interest, are becoming increasingly like an overall life tax for humans that are farmed to make other people richer. Seven Plums is a romantic and ideal example of another way. We really can spend a whole day cooking dinner instead of shopping our way into an abyss. Not only does Li Ziqi enjoy the near-meditative/peaceful state of growing, collecting, and cooking food, but there is also a clear financial benefit to doing it all yourself (for free).

The millions of people who watch her videos every day must dream of having a life like hers. Maybe they think it's an impossible dream? I think we only have to step back in time a few years, before the internet took control of our lives, and start our lives all over again. Most of us have grandfathers and grandmothers who baked the most delicious bread, grew tomatoes and pumpkins in the backyard, made delicious lemonade and ginger beer, made their clothes, made and fixed everything themselves, and enjoyed time on the front porch just... relaxing (maybe eating butter pecan ice cream). How do you value your life these days? Are you running from one bill to the next? Are you feeling like life is out of control? Do you want a better life? If so, I would recommend watching all the Seven Plums videos until your soul jumpstarts you back into the future.

Home

Owning a home is our biggest challenge, our biggest debt, our biggest interest payment or loss, and the biggest reason we keep fighting to stay in our jobs. On average (USA, 2019), we pay $169,390 in interest over a 30-year home loan, or around $5,645 a year. Quite a few years ago, I bought some land beside a forest, pulled down an old brick home in a nearby town, and rebuilt it in a different way on my land. This was labor-intensive and very cheap to build. In this age of millennials, it is more likely that people would rather put all their time into the internet and would not be interested in months of hard work. Hard work never killed anyone, and I would argue that 12 months of hard work building or renovating your own home at weekends is "less work" than paying back $169,390 in interest over 30 long years. I am forever reminded of Mick Jagger singing, "Think of all the good times I've been wasting, having good times." In many ways, this is my mantra. I don't like fun, or shopping, or drinking, or talking, or traveling, or debt, or anything that takes me away from finding my inner bliss.

There are many alternatives to buying a big new home and paying it off for 30 years (these days, people refinance their homes so they are never paid off, adding even more interest). These options include building your own home out of recycled materials, either by yourself or with some help. Renovating an old warehouse or house (reducing interest and time on your loan or making it easier and quicker to save money to buy it) using your own labor building a granny flat at the back of your parent's house (1 bedroom), and when they get old and you have children, swap houses. Maybe you can live on a boat or in a lighthouse. In Southeast Asia, many families live together. They have large building blocks, and when their children marry, they build a home next door but on the same land as their parents. Their culture is quite different from Western culture: they love family and want to stay together, support, and love each other forever. They often share food, transport, tools, equipment, and labor. Westerners are often on their own because they seek independence and freedom from family, but at what cost? There is a huge price to pay for independence and freedom, which includes emotional, financial, and intellectual costs. Often in Asia, when people get married, they live with her or his parents. This is normally a joy and is certainly a more sustainable lifestyle. So, for Westerners to own their own home, I suggest they become more Asian and truly love their families, rejoice in them, and be happy. The benefits are enormous. You can save money for your new house, you can build on the same land, you can get help building your home, and you will never be lonely again.

In places like Australia and England, you could build a one-bedroom granny flat in your parent's backyard, live happily and debt-free, and when you have your children, you can swap houses and take care of each other forever and ever. If you are thinking "no way," then think again.

It is not hard for a woman or a man to learn how to renovate a building. I enjoy this kind of work and feel immense pride when I see the results. Again, decide between hard work or higher debt. For the past two decades, more and more people have chosen professions like lawyering and teaching. Not many people want a normal "trades-style" job anymore. Is it because of the money? A bricklayer can earn more than a teacher. Is it because of the hard work? Yes, I think it is. More and more men don't like hard work and prefer to play on their computers. I don't agree with this thinking. Learning a trade like carpentry gives you enormous skills that will benefit you for a lifetime. Hard work is a gym in disguise: you get paid to do a workout. In the past, I built my own home, and the skills I learned doing that have been with me every day since. I cannot imagine not having the skills I have: bricklaying, concreting, carpentry, tiling, painting, and plumbing. If you choose to build a granny flat, a recycled home, or renovate an old building, not only will you save thousands of dollars, but your debt will be short-lived.

Health

Healthcare is incredibly expensive, whether you have insurance or not. Medical fees in places like the US are astronomical and rising. The long list of payments you make in a month is headed by your home, your car, and your health insurance. These three alone can wipe out your monthly income. If you build a small house and maybe ride a motorcycle, then the next step is to buy a book on herbs. Herbs, along with exercise and diet, are the best form of preventative health care. Common herbs like ginger and turmeric are cheap and increase your health every day you take them. Regular exercise is a proven way to stay healthy into your 70s. My brother is 80 and recently came second in the world cycling championships in Austria. Diet is also such an easy way to keep yourself away from expensive doctors and hospitals. Organic food (fruit, vegetables, beans, and nuts), good water, clean air, and plenty of sunshine all make a huge difference.

Yoga and meditation reduce your stress levels. Stress is the number-one cause of disease. When I am stressed, I get the flu more often and am less careful about what I eat and drink. Health is a natural state well into your 90s if you follow these simple steps. not too much meat, some dark chocolate, and red wine. Plenty of vegetables like sweet potatoes and broccoli Eat every kind of fruit you can, especially in season. Nuts and seeds are something you should eat every day. Olive and avocado oils are good. Do some exercise every day: you can work in your organic vegetable garden, go for a walk or a swim, or paint your house. Spend time with friends and family and feel happy all over.

Disease is double pain: it's expensive and painful.

CBD Oil is a miracle cure for many diseases, like cancer. It is finally legal in many states and countries and should be the first thing you take if you are unwell. You can do the research on the internet. Many doctors now recommend CBD oil for complaints like cancer, Parkinson's disease, and arthritis. This is an easy herb to trust because the research is in and doctors support it.

Other health issues, like dentistry, can be expensive too. Of course, prevention is better than cure when it comes to your teeth. So, be mindful of your teeth and keep them in "checkup condition" rather than a "filling" one. Some people swear by coconut oil as a way to keep their teeth and gums healthy. If you search "coconut oil pulling" on the internet, there are a lot of articles. You decide if it's a good idea or not.

Mental health can be expensive to treat, too, with psychiatrists and therapists. In Southeast Asia, people don't have time to become crazy or depressed; they must work every day to buy food. They also have the continual, unconditional, loving support of family always nearby. Westerners are plagued with confusion and doubt, which leads to wrong thinking. Again, in Southeast Asia, everyone says, "Don't think too much." They like meditation and prayer and follow the Buddhist path—the middle way. The middle way, or path, is about keeping yourself in balance, especially your emotions. One way to do this is to try to feel peaceful and calm and not be angered or overcome with desire.

Many of the topics in this book require you to change your life. Maybe you will change it a lot or a little, but the most important thing is that you do change it because it is normal for the better: less debt, less interest, greater health, and happiness.

Richard Arvin Overton

Yeah I've had a lot of people say God kept you here to help others but I don't know why he kept me here I can't tell you. I ain't talked to Him and He ain't he talked to me.

My name is Richard Arvin Overton I am a hundred and nine years old. I still walk, I still talk and I still drive. I just got my license renewed this year. They give me an eye test. Everything they give me now I pass it. I feel good going on driving. I like to drive myself 'cause other drivers, they drive crazy.

I am the oldest World War II veteran. I went in the Army at 1940. Made you more braver, stronger, I can sleep with every door open here without a lock on it. Ain't scared, no. Ain't nothing gonna bother you. You see a soldier with a gun you don't see him turn around and go back this way. He may go sideways… but he ain't gonna turn around and go back. Don't care how hot them bullets is, he ain't gonna go back. So when you go in there you just say, well God has got me now. See… He gonna take care of you. If it's your time to go then that bullet is going to get ya. If it ain't your time to go, that bullet's going over your head, it ain't gonna to hit you So, man will kill you but God is the one keep you alive. It wasn't good but we had to go.

I built me a house in 1945 and that's where I have been ever since. It's a nice place to live. Yeah I'm happy with my house. It's all I need. I would buy one thing, I would use that one thing. I wouldn't buy one thing and go buy another and and go buy another. I've got a truck out there and it runs just like I want it, so I just keep it. But I don't fool with a credi card, never. For everything I get I pay cash for it. I got 50 cents a day, that's way back yonder. But I lived out of that. Of course everything was nickel and dime, three cents. I remember when a man had the first Ford, I was at… Working in the… I think I was picking cotton down there and we heard that he was gonna get a car. We didn't know what a car was, we'd heard about it, but we would never come to town much. My first car was a little old Ford,

Model T Ford. Had to get in front and crank it. You remember them, Oh no you wasn't born then was you? No…. I know you wasn't.

I just sit there and sometimes smoke 12 cigars a day, sometimes more than that. Anybody say "what do you smoke em for?" I just, it just, it makes you feel better. But you can't inhale. Best to go ahead and just blow it out and let it go and forget about swallowing it. If you swallow it, ain't no taste to it; it just makes you cough. I'm doing it the healthyy way.

Every time I get up in the morning that cat is sitting there waiting. And either I go to bed sometimes they're sitting there waiting 'cause they wanna get their supper and then they wanna go to bed. But you don't feed a cat too much 'cause he won't eat a rat. I help those cats and they keep me happy. I… I tell the truth they keep me happy, I wanna see my cats every morning.

I wake up at 1 either wake up at 2 or 3… anytime I wake up I just get up. I get me a cup of coffee. Sometimes I drink about four cups of coffee in the morning. This morning I drank about that much whiskey.

I love milk, and fish, corn and soup; I love soup. A lot of people don't like soup and don't drink milk, but I been drinking milk for over… practically all my life. And ice cream. I eat ice cream every night: it makes me happy. I eat butter pecan. If you wanna buy any, you buy butter pecan. And it's the Overton Diet: it's anybody's diet that wanna eat it.

Church is a wonderful place, lovely place. Keeps me goin' makes me feel good. I think that helps me push myself along going to church. You learn something at church too. You learn how to live better; how to treat people. We don't have all the answers, I got to save some of the answers for somebody else to do. And singing, I love that church singing: beautiful. Church is just for everybody. But, you gotta go for one person, that's yourself. Good to have a spiritual life: but you got to live it. It makes …. It makes you feel better.

To have a person around you like MS Love; we get along real nice. Oh, she's 91 years old: you know I'm 109. And yeah, we go to the hospital to see people. We go to the grocery store, we go shopping sometimes. I take her to church, and take her different places, she's just a nice person. Yeah, we have fun together.

I've seen lots and lots of living. But I am still living good; I ain't suffered or nothing. I gets what I want. So, I'm still living alright. If you give up you're through! You just doubting yourself. I am, I'm giving you some of my secrets to a long life: if you ever use it. If you don't use it that's your bad luck. My time ain't got here yet. And I don't know when I come here and I don't know when I'm going. You either… neither one of us know when we going.

I may give out but I never give up.

Bartering

In trade, barter, which comes from the word "baretor," is an exchange system in which goods or services are directly traded for other goods or services without the use of a medium of exchange, like money.

A few decades ago, before the internet, there were local trading schemes where people signed up as members, offered different products and services, and traded them for services and products they needed. They often used tokens, which, like money, represented the value they were giving and receiving. Now, 20 years later, we have the internet, where bartering is universal and easy. So, why barter? The main reason is that we all have skills and products that, though not commercially viable, are still in demand from other people in our neighborhood, whether physically or virtually. This gives normal people who can't afford to advertise or rent a shop the "power" to trade. Bartering is the best way to improve our lives and get what we want without paying someone else to do it.

Bartering is back now that cash is no longer king. In the past year, trading activity on Craigslist alone has increased by 100%, and dozens of new websites are springing up to connect eager swappers. Traders exchange services as diverse as photography, gymnastics classes, and babysitting to save hundreds, and often even thousands, of dollars. You can obtain comparable financial benefits—and even more—by heeding the counsel of seasoned barterers. "Bartering is about communities, thus there is a psychological advantage. Human interaction is encouraged.

Interest and Debt

From the moment we're born, we're taught that borrowing money is normal and, dare I say it, expected. From mortgages to car loans to the $700 smartphones we pay for over 24 months, we're taught to spread the pain of our purchases for many months or years.

Sometimes debt is a good thing when you want to study, buy a home or a car, or start a new business. But the cost of debt is high—much higher than we think. The interest on a typical home loan can be as much as $6,000 a year. When you buy a new car, you will pay $900 a year in interest. Another form of debt is a credit card. The average interest paid on credit cards is $800. Student loans average out at $700 for 10 years. If you also borrow money for smartphones, furniture, and electronic goods, your total interest for a year is around $10,000. This is without actually paying back any of the capital on the loans—just interest.

Buying smaller, cheaper things and saving money will allow you to manage your debt and pay things off much quicker; maybe you won't have any debt at all if you do what Mr. Overton does and pay cash for everything and keep it forever. I have friends who have been paying back a car loan for six years and cannot afford a pizza.

Our lives don't have to be like this if we follow these 10 golden rules. Pay cash, save money, do it yourself, keep it forever, barter, ride a bike, grow your own, keep it small, team up with your parents, and be healthy.

Riding a bike

For the past 10 years, I have been riding a Honda Wave motorcycle. I do have an old Toyota when I need a car; it costs around $1000. When I drive the car, I worry about the cost of fuel and all the noises coming from under the car. The Honda is a different story. It costs $5 to fill, it never needs fixing, and the fun of turning into a curve with the air in your face is priceless.

When I was 18, I bought an old Triumph Tiger that had no front brakes; I didn't know until I ended up in the hospital. I was riding with a friend who was in front of me, and the lights would go dimmer the faster I went. He stopped in front of me because he could not see my lights. I immediately jammed on my brakes (I only had the back ones), and the bike rolled to the right and then to the left, which catapulted me through the air past the disbelieving eyes of my friend and into the grass on the side of the road. I lay there moaning for five minutes with my friend in panic when an army convoy going past stopped, lifted me into the back of a truck, and took me to the hospital; luckily, no serious damage had been done. This was my second bike accident. I had one on the way to work in a big city. I was riding in the left lane, and a big concrete mixer truck was in front of me and on my right in the right lane. Suddenly it decided to turn left down a side street, and I went under it. The bike and I were pushed along the road by the back wheel; luckily, it never rolled over me. The driver stopped quickly, too. When the truck stopped, I was lying under the back wheel, entangled in my motorcycle, with assorted cuts and bruises. I had a silver ring that was bent and jammed into my finger that hurt. Soon enough, an ambulance came, and I was in the hospital getting stitched up. The night before, I had slept at my friend's house. He waved me goodbye in the morning and wished me luck with my new job. Roughly four hours later, I returned to his house covered in bandages, blood, and torn clothes. How lucky was that?

It took around 40 years before I was back on a bike again. I have fallen off a couple of times without serious injury over the past ten years. I love motorcycles. They have been poor people's transport for decades: bikes are so much fun, one of the many times it's good not to be rich.

Food

In some countries, you can spend an enormous amount of money on food, especially if you buy it from a supermarket.

The merchant has easy access to your hard-earned money when you buy food. One of the best ways to save money and be healthier is to grow and make your own food. Italians are famous for their homemade wine, sausage, and pasta. They are also known to have wonderful vegetable gardens full of rich, ripe tomatoes, dark green bushes of basil, and plump buds of garlic. I admire this lifestyle and wish I could get off the computer sometimes and copy it.

There are many things you can do for yourself when it comes to food, like Seven Plums and the Italians. I love to make sourdough bread and ginger beer. Pizzas are fun too.

If you are feeling poor and stressed, then get out your shovel and some chicken manure and become half Chinese and half Italian. You will save a lot of money, enjoy delicious, fresh food, and feel relaxed and peaceful all at the same time.

There is something wrong with our lives when we are always paying for things. Fuel for the car, clothes, food, medicine, doctors, rent, tax, interest, schools... When we pay, it always makes someone else rich: the merchant. We live in capitalist monetary systems that support the rich and annihilate the poor. Everyone in the middle is trying to climb higher and higher to get away from annihilation. The only way out is to stop spending and do it all yourself. Don't buy anything. Make it, grow it, and find it.

In Southeast Asia, most poor people follow these rules, survive, and live happy lives. They help each other build their homes. They grow rice and fruit to eat, and they find herbs, leaves, and mushrooms in the fields and forests. They also catch fish in their rice fields and waterways.

If you search the internet for edible leaves, you will be shocked.

Around 50% of all leaves are edible. Some of them are herbal and have curative properties. Papaya leaves cure malaria, and mango leaves reduce blood sugar levels. A lot of food can be grown at home, but you can also scavenge for wild food that grows in nearby fields and forests. I often think that in English-speaking countries that were populated by poor people from Great Britain, we have a "drink beer and eat oats" mentality. We are oblivious to the wondrous world around us that is overflowing with goodies we can eat and drink.

There are so many good examples of how people live a more sustainable, self-sufficient lifestyle. Again, search the internet for information about Italian food. Look at all the Seven Plums videos on YouTube. Search for edible leaves and herbs on all continents. Learn how to make bread, cheese, beer, and wine. Say no to the merchants who are sitting in a shop somewhere, waiting to take your money.

Maybe I sound a bit alternative when I talk about these subjects. But if you think about it... What's wrong with growing and making your food? It will be more delicious and healthier. This is more than just saving money. It is about health, happiness, and balance. It will also be helpful in any kind of crash or disaster that may come our way in the future.

Equivalent wages

$100 in 1972 is equivalent in purchasing power to $574.18 in 2016, a difference of $474.18 over 44 years.

Back in 1972, we were earning more than four times what we are earning now. One reason for this dramatic drop in real income is that women are entering the workforce in large numbers. This took the pressure off men's wages, as a husband and wife now had two incomes. It has all been downhill since then. I remember that a single man could go to work, provide for his family, buy a car, and buy a house back then. Now, family life is often a scramble to survive with both parents working. How did this happen? It happened because business people hate paying people for their work, period. Only a few companies want to share their profits with their workers.

Recently, my brother said that the economic situation is very bad. Families with two people working cannot pay their electric bills, their car registration, and all their other monthly and yearly bills. Wages are 14 of what they were in 1972, so how could they? How can we? 99% of people in the US have less than $1000 in savings. If our wages are so bad, it's time to take action and find every way we can to save money and have a good life. The Italians must be the first step.

Clothes

Clothing, especially from China, is pretty cheap, but if you have a large family, clothes are expensive. My mother loved her sewing machine and making hats and shirts. She didn't have to; she had plenty of money as she got older, but memories of a poor childhood kept her sewing into her 70s. When I was in my thirties, I knew a lot of people who bought wool fresh off the sheep's back and spun it into balls of wool with a spinning wheel. Around the same time, I met people who made leather shoes and handbags. It was common to see people sitting around a log fire knitting jumpers or sewing a handbag.

The Seven Plums channel has some videos on making and dying clothes. This book is about living cheaply, living better, and reducing our exposure to the digital world. If you decide to make the change, then there is an infinite amount of information on the internet to help you on your way. Making ginger beer is more fun than watching soap operas on TV—that's how I feel. If you turn your life around by 90 degrees, you will see what I see. A beautiful world, wonderful people, amazing landscapes, and a huge variety of food were all given to us by what people call God. I thank this God every day for the love and happiness, for the breathtaking beauty, and for the paradise, we wake up to every day. Our spiritual lives can lead us to happiness much more than money ever could or can.

Summary

There is so much more to living a debt-free life than what I have written in this small book. The internet has everything you need. We are all paying interest, tax, and bills, and other people are enjoying large profits. For those of us who are normal and work hard for every dollar, it is stressful and wrong. If we sit down and add up all the hidden costs that we pay every month, we will know why life is not easy. When I make things myself, I feel a timeless sense of pride and joy. When I am paying for things every 60 minutes, I yearn for a better way. In Southeast Asia, when people have problems, they say they will go to the temple and become monks. They say monks have no worries because they get a free home, free food, and free education and health care. I think it's time we all became monks in our own homes. Walk a peaceful path, feel at one with the universe, and enjoy all the simple things in life that are free or nearly so.

Let me think of the many free things: swimming, walking, running, sleeping, working, writing, drawing, kissing, hugging, a God, the act of cooking, dancing, singing, thinking, dreaming, speaking, making, looking, smelling, loving, teaching, listening, meditating, yoga, climbing, playing, learning, gaining wisdom, forgiveness, compassion, kindness, giving, taking, sharing, drinking, eating, growing, and changing.

I am tired of the billionaires and millionaires because there should not be one person on this planet going hungry or suffering in any way. Prosperity consciousness is about prosperity for all, not just one or two.

Thank you for buying this small book. I hope it helps.

Roditch

roditch@protonmail.com